EQUILIBRIUM

What Makes People Do Things They Shouldn't Do

MANHARDEEP SINGH

PREFACE

It is so common to misunderstand someone's action or just reacting without understanding why someone might have done something. I too was one among them, when ultimately I decided to change my POV (Point-Of-View). I tried to look through other's eyes to get the answer of why they would have done something which is bothering me. To my surprise, whenever I contemplated about this, I always got the answer, and most of the times, finding this answer brought more peace in my life than it would have if I didn't bother to change my perception.

To explain it in a better way, let me share with you a story. Once, there lived a couple in a house. The wife kept complaining about the neighbor's dirty clothes. She kept complaining, "That lady doesn't know how to wash clothes properly. She doesn't even have proper eye sight to see that the clothes are still dirty." This incident repeated for a couple of days when finally one day she said with a smile, "Well, seems like someone finally taught her how to wash clothes." Her husband looked towards her and said, "Honey, nobody taught her how to wash clothes. I just cleaned our house's window."

Many a times, we are looking through the dirty window and feel that other person is wrong. Try cleaning the window and change your POV to understand a situation better.

Take a look at the following picture. It is impossible to say who is right. But it is true that for both of them the other person will remain wrong until they step out from their shoes and look at the number from other's point of view.

With this aim, to help people understand each other better and to bring harmony in their relationships, EQUILIBRIUM has come into existence.

To help us comprehend the context in a better way, I would be taking assistance of graphology (commonly known as handwriting analysis). With handwriting analysis, you will be able to deduce what makes someone do things which according to you they shouldn't do.

WHY THIS BOOK?

There had been various times when I heard someone complain about their parents, siblings, best friend or just someone who keeps bothering them. All I hear every time is the complaining and how annoying it is for them to deal with it. Surprisingly, no one actually is thinking about finding a solution. A solution that can create a win-win possibility for both the parties. A solution that can be accepted by the complainer without trying to change the one who is bothering. After all, it is a fact that you can't change anyone in the world but you.

The easiest solution to this problem is to look at the world from their perspective. Doing so may help us realize that they were right at what they do. This book is an attempt to inset such insights that can help understand this in a clearer way.

THE BOOK STRUCTURE

To be able to get the most out of the book, even as a lay reader, the book has various chapters, each defining a separate personality trait which you may find in your life. Along with the personality trait will be some insight into what may make them do what they normally shouldn't.

All the personality traits are accompanied with graphical examples of handwriting samples for easy understanding on how the handwriting stroke pertaining to a particular personality trait actually looks like.

Lastly:

DISCLAIMER – The author is not liable for any damage or harm done from the information contained here within. The information contained in this book is purely educational, obtained from personal experience and knowledge from various books.

CONTENTS

1. INTRODUCTION

THE GOAL OF A MOVE

Before we start learning about what makes people do things they shouldn't do, it is important to understand why someone would do something at the first place. Take an example of touching a hot pan. As soon as you feel the hotness, your body's reflex action kicks in and the hand is automatically pulled away. You didn't even do anything, then why such a move? It is a defense mechanism of the body to protect you from harm.

What happens when you are afraid or when you are doing an adventure sport, say bungee jumping, for instance? Your heart starts pounding against your ribs. Your senses get better. This is a "fight of flight" mode (no no not airplane mode) of your body. The body releases adrenaline hormone that prepares the body for action. This too is not under your control. It too is a defense mechanism of the body for survival. There might be so many other defense mechanisms of the body like these that help with our survival, whether it is white blood cells who work to fight bacteria or the platelets that clog off a cut, one thing is clear - they all are meant to keep us alive.

Think about this: what would happen if these defense mechanisms didn't exist? We would be dead before we know it.

So, it can be inferred that the ultimate goal of a move or an action is survival.

AN UNCONSCIOUS CONDITIONING

It is also important to consider that not only is any action related to the survival of the being, but most of the times, it is triggered unconsciously. For instance, if a child fails in exams and his parents give him a chocolate thinking that it may make him feel better, what they are actually doing is conditioning him that every time you fail, you will receive a chocolate, a reward. They are preparing him for failure. Too often, this small gesture goes long way affecting how we work and act.

Consider this, if you are a foreigner and you come to India, the first thing which will annoy you the most is the honking of horns. In western countries, honking a horn is deemed to be cursing, while in India it is too common that a person may even honk a horn before he starts his vehicle (well, I exaggerated a little there). But the point is, when you are put in a new situation, a new environment, your body starts looking for ways of survival. It starts releasing hormones, creates changes to adapt to the new environment.

It is all at last an unconscious conditioning.

CHILDHOOD EXPERIENCES

Believe it or not, most of us do what we do because of

our childhood conditioning. It is said in the same context that a child's mind is like wet cement, whatever falls on it, leaves an impression. Take the story of a circus elephant. A circus elephant has such tremendous strength that it can uproot a giant tree, but still it keeps standing once it is chained to a stomp (and sometimes even the stump doesn't exist). The elephant has the power to simply move and break the chains, but why doesn't it move? It doesn't break-free because of its childhood experience.

When that elephant was small, it was chained with a strong chain. At that time, it tried to break-free itself. Tried too hard for too long but nothing seemed to work. Finally, the elephant gave up and got conditioned that once these chains are around its leg, it can't move freely.

We are no different, it is just that we may not be able to digest this truth but we do have these invisible chains chained to our legs. We are product of our childhood experiences.

THE DEFENSE MECHANISM

Coming back to the point, what makes someone do something they shouldn't do? It is definitely an action/move which is most of the time triggered through an unconscious, at times, childhood conditioning. But why or when does this get triggered? That is where the stimuli – the environment, the situation, the equation between two people, comes into play.

Whenever a situation arises where a fear is perceived, the body and mind starts to act in the defensive way. With fears come defensive mechanisms. If you have a fear of being attacked, you would somehow prepare yourself to defend against the attack. That is what the body and mind does too.

For instance, if you were to build a castle in a hostile territory/environment, you will have to build a moat; you will also have guns, spears and fire to assist you in protection. But you only need these defenses if you are in a hostile environment. If you know you are in a safe area and had no fear of getting attacked, you would not need any of those defenses.

In a similar fashion, personality too has its own defence mechanism. This mechanism helps in reaching a point of equilibrium, where there is no fear of survival and is a place of healthy development. Take that harmonious situation away, and the personality goes into disequilibrium for which it finds ways to get back to the equilibrium.

HE IS THE PROBLEM, NOT ME!

If you keep having this thought in your mind that the other person is the problem and not me, then you yourself are in problem. It is popularly quoted "It's not what happens to you, but how you react to it, that matters." Tough situations will come. You will meet many more tough people – in the form of clients, seniors, bosses, juniors, colleagues, strangers, co-passengers, store owners, flight attendant etc. You may not like what they do or how they do something but if you let yourself upset over those things, then you need to lighten your burden a bit. Take life a little less seriously. Try seeing the situation from their eyes. EQUILIBRIUM will help you in doing that.

2. WHY GRAPHOLOGY?

I am sure you might have this question in your mind since reading the preface – "Why are you taking the assistance of graphology?" or a simpler (Lite) version of the question, "Why graphology?"

I am using graphology for two simple things:

• It is easy to obtain someone's handwriting.
• It is a proven science, with many years of research.

You can pinpoint a personality trait from its handwriting stroke and answer why he is that way. This is exactly what we will be doing in this book. We will learn various reasons that may cause someone to act differently or in weird fashion, whether it is a trait of introversion and shyness or a tendency to suicide, we will learn what makes them behave and do that which we feel that they shouldn't do.

3. THE LOW-SPIRITED

I bet you might have met a low-spirited in your life, they are so many in numbers, and they are everywhere. This is the personality trait where whatever you do, they'll feel bad and in low spirits. They will drag their feet wherever they go and have slouch in the back. Whenever they have a new opportunity, they see the negative first, giving reasons why it can't be done. Generally, they stay in a bad situation or relationship for a long time and are not able to move on. They believe that they deserve bad so they never even try to look at the ray of light at the far end. Usually, when they look in the mirror they see the imperfections in them despite their achievements.

If you are friends with a low-spirited personality, you will observe that they will need a constant reassurance that what they are doing is right and the people around them accept them.

THE TRAIT:

In graphology and psychology, these are the symptoms of a person who has a very low self-esteem. Self-esteem, a high one, is considered as one of the primary traits found in the handwriting of successful people. In the book, 14 Strokes of Billionaires, high self-esteem is the first and the most widely found trait in the handwriting of successful people.

The low-spirited is just the opposite, he has low self-esteem and is not able to see the positive side and there is a reason for that. There is a reason why he acts all hopeless and finds reasons why something can't be done. Let's take a look at them.

In handwriting, low self-esteem is depicted by a low crossing t-bar (horizontal line). Here is how it looks:

THE REASON:

The primary reason why they are not hopeful of the future is because of their fear. They have a fear of failure. In the past, they might have experienced repetitive failure or a major setback because of which they are afraid to feel that pain again. They aren't ready to endure that pain and don't want to experience the stress of risk that involves in voyaging your way to betterment.

This fear of failure is also the reason why they constantly look for reassurance. The past setback has left its impression so deep in the mind that they can't get it out of their mind. It has become so accustomed in the system that they don't even realize that it exists. So whenever an opportunity comes in front of them, the fear of failure triggers in and they start looking at ways why something won't work.

It is also because of this past failure that they aren't able to let go of people or situations that are bad for them. In my experience, I have seen a girl being used as a doormat by a guy, while she never left him. She used to wait for him for hours and all he did was come and scold her. Why wouldn't you leave such a guy? Why wouldn't you move on? Because there is fear that if they move on then the future will be even worse.

HOW TO HANDLE A LOW-SPIRITED:

To bring the personality back to equilibrium and keep it there, you need to keep reassuring them and recommend exercises or activities related to self-esteem. The best and the easiest one is to keep chanting "I AM THE BEST". Initially, the words may not come out from the mouth but once it becomes a habit, it will start to rewire the mind and changes will start happening.

To understand this situation even better, imagine there are two buckets – one with black paint and one with white. The low-spirited has black paint bucket – full of hopelessness and negativity. The goal is to turn this black paint to white. The only feasible solution to this is adding more and more white paint (positivity) to it until black paint has vanished.

4. THE SUPER-SENSITIVE

Another personality which you might have met in life is the super-sensitive. They are the people who take everything to heart. They are passionate, no doubt, but at times become passionate about unnecessary stuff, such as being upset that they missed the first show of their favorite actor's new movie. Not only just that, they will be upset for it for months, and sometimes even years! No kidding!

THE TRAIT:

In handwriting analysis, this trait is called the same – high sensitivity. It is common to see this trait in passionate people or people who get aggressive very easily. They make use of force and energy to get things done. They put in their strength in everything they do, including writing something; that is why their handwriting sample is made up of heavy pen strokes. In layman's language, you would be able to see the impression of what they write on even the 4th or 5th page of the notebook. Imagine whom are you dealing with if the paper tears up with the writing of the person. My advice: RUN!

9

Here is the sample of a heavy pressure writer:

See the path that this plane takes, and the trail that it makes. With your finger, follow the line and trace the trail from side to side.

THE REASON:

The reason why some people are so sensitive is because they put in their heart and more into what they do. To get the thing done successfully, they put in a lot of force and energy. Because they put in their heart to everything they do, they also take everything to heart. They don't take things casually, they can't. In such a situation, an unfit and non-serious person is surely going to be the target of a sensitive person's rage.

HOW TO HANDLE A SUPER-SENSITIVE:

Since they put in a lot of energy in what they do, it is best to avoid at the first place. Keep things straight. Watch your words. You might be cracking a light joke, which a sensitive person may take very seriously. Just don't mess with sensitive people because the misuse of the force they put in the work can make the writer a threat to others or to himself. There is an excess of force they have in them.

If you are a heavy writer and get really aggressive too easily, its best to find a healthy outlet of your excessive energy. Gym, yoga, exercise, jogging, anger management programs etc are good options to choose from.

5. THE IMPULSIVE

Admit it: we all have experienced how impulsive people can be. Even before you have finished speaking the sentence, they would react. They are quick at showing emotions, whether its laughter, love, cry or hate, they can easily and quickly portray it. Their eyes speak, and so does their body. If you are a keen observer with a little knowledge about body language, you could tell what they are up to without even listening to them. They are that expressive. And because they are that expressive, they are hard to be around. Who likes to be around a ticking time-bomb who can go off any minute with just a small bad news?

THE TRAIT:

The impulsive are nothing but hyper-expressive personalities. They are apt to be around people and express freely. They love expressing and think more from their heart than from their brain; that is why they are the ones who get easily disappointed as well. In handwriting, high degree of emotional expressiveness can be categorized with a hard rightward slant of the handwriting

– a handwriting which is almost going to fall flat towards the right. Here is a graphical example:

People who love to eat are always the best people.

THE REASON:

The impulsive people are people-oriented. People are more important than anything for them. They react weird or hysterically because of insecurity and jealousy. They have a fear of being left alone. Having no one around them is their worst nightmare, and they are ready to go to any limit to prevent this from happening. They try to be entertaining when they can and at the same time will openly express disappointments and sadness when something hurts them.

Since they are insecure, almost all the times they are not in control of the situation. To tell you the truth, they are not even in control of how they behave; it is but the stimulus, the outer environment that actually controls it. Quite dangerous!

As already said they are less rational and more excitable. They don't simply want people in their life; they depend upon them for ego-support and for guidelines in building their own self-image. Most of the times, they are unconsciously trying to pickup cues on how they "should" act from what they sense as the approval or disapproval of people around them.

In an extreme scenario, they can latch onto someone with a smothering grip, and can therefore sometimes be forcibly rejected. It is but in their nature to get over-involved, over-stimulated and over-excited. And the problem is that they don't really know what it is they are running to, they just know they want to get there in the fastest way possible.

HOW TO HANDLE AN IMPULSIVE:

This is bit tricky, because whatever you do, you are going to get a reaction. Understand that they are doing all that for a reason – and that is getting accepted and being involved. It is important to them to make sure they are not "left out" of anything, so try involving them. Trust me, they might be exhausting to live with, and it's difficult if not impossible to explain to them that they are actively alienating themselves by the intensity of their emotional demands. Just compare the brute emotional force to get what you want with chopping an onion. It needs control, otherwise you risk yourself chopping off your finger or hurting yourself.

6. THE COLD FAÇADE

There are personalities who seem very cold and heartless. Their face remains the same in every situation – expressionless. They are just the extreme opposite of "THE IMPULSIVE". While an impulsive may shout and tell everyone whenever he is impressed, the cold façade would remain composed, even if he is impressed. Many people judge them as heartless or someone who doesn't understand emotions, but to be true, they are all wrong. These people too, feel every emotion. Then why don't they express it, you may ask? Well, there is a reason behind it.

They prefer to work alone and enjoy time when aloof. They do feel the emotions but they don't express it until they become extreme or build up over time, such as extreme anger, passion or stress.

I recently got in contact with a junior of mine from high school. She was very calm and composed when we initially started talking. After about 3 months, she revealed that she was super excited to talk to me, but didn't show in her expressions that time. Yes, these people do exist.

THE TRAIT:

The cold-façade has a trait complete opposite to that of the impulsive. If the impulsive are extremely emotionally expressive, the cold façade are emotionally withdrawn. In handwriting analysis too, they are the opposite of the impulsive, as their handwriting falls towards the left side of the page. Here is an example:

THE REASON:

As already said, the cold façade personalities do feel every emotion, it is just that they do not express it, and they don't express the emotions because they have a fear of expressing themselves, they have a fear of getting hurt. Apparently, this fear has developed either overtime or by getting a big blow from someone whom the writer was really close to emotionally. Whatever the reason is, it is evident that they have fear of getting hurt again so prefer to have a cold face rather than a bleeding heart.

Recent research has also revealed that most of these leftward slant writers suffered a profound physical or sexual trauma when they were children, and the result was a compromised ability to open up and trust people. As they experienced the trauma, they developed issues as a child with feeling safe and expressing their emotions. So in order to cope up with that and be in equilibrium they withdraw into oneself for emotional support and security.

HOW TO DEAL WITH THE COLD FAÇADE:

Since these writers tend to be judged by others as cold,

15

uninvolved and uncaring. It is quite easy to locate them. They find outgoing behaviour uncomfortable. Such writers are very cautious in establishing relationships with others and they feel isolated in crowds. They find it difficult to communicate and difficult to trust others. In such a scenario, it is best to keep at bay and let them make a move. Give them time to be comfortable. If they think you deserve to be close to them then you will come to know, otherwise, just move on.

Usually they are dealing with a problem in communication: These writers often can't tell anyone how they feel, they are certain that they will be misunderstood, and because of their reticence often are, which only adds to their feelings of rejection. So their rejection is what makes them going back to themselves rather than to other people. Do not reject them. Help them come out of their shell. Make them feel comfortable around people. But make sure you do not over-do it. They are very suspicious, so a behaviour too caring and helping may be perceived as selfish motive and they may shut you out of their inner circle.

7. THE PRESENT-LIVER

If you are a party freak, you can easily point towards the person in your gang who has the best time in the party, with whom the party just goes to the next level- that is the present liver. They have the best parties. They have it because they live in the present. They are not bothered by future thoughts or the consequences, they just know that there is one moment to live and that is right now, and they function on this thought every day.

Apparently, people call them with various names but the most common one is "you are so immature" and indeed they are. They can behave childish if they want to because they don't really care what the consequences will be. Basically, they are lead by their libido, the pleasure hormone. So they are apt to choose an option which will give them more pleasure and fun. For instance, if they are given a choice between taking final exams and hanging out with friends, they will choose the latter. Did you just say "crazy"? Not crazy, they do exist.

THE TRAIT:

This personality is known as the person who lives in the moment. In handwriting analysis, there are different zones which can easily say whether a person is more intellectual, sensual or just want to live life. This personality trait is depicted when the height of the big letters such as "h, t, d, k, b" etc is equal to the height of small letters such as "m, n, a, c, e" etc. Here is the example:

THE REASON:

The main reason why they are like that is because to these writers the social acceptance means more than any other kind of personal achievement. It is a characteristic of the handwriting of children. Just as the young child is primarily concerned with emotional security and the approval of authority (in the form of parents and teachers and other significant adults) these writers do look for such approvals and social acceptances. This type of writing is an unquestionable sign of mental, emotional and even physical immaturity.

HOW TO DEAL WITH PRESENT LIVER:

Since they are similar to children, they should be handled carefully, but most of the times if you want to get them to do something, simply show them how much fun they will get when they will do it, and they will do it. Give them social approval when they need one. When you give this approval, they would be more than happy to be around you.

8. THE HARSH WORDER

Do you know someone who can almost kill someone with their words? Someone who is good at throwing curve balls during a conversation and get you in a corner? Someone who if poked can literally strip you down to bones with their words? Who can harass as well as embarrass you while keeping themselves high? The harsh worder is the personality trait in which a person adepts to saying harshly, mostly in a double-meaning sarcastic way to hurt someone or else mock someone. Simply said, they use sarcasm to say something but mean something else.

THE TRAIT:

The trait that describes the harsh worder personality is sarcasm. It is not ironical that even in handwriting analysis, the concerned stroke which depicts sarcasm looks just like the tongue of a sarcastic person – a dagger. In a simpler sense, sarcasm is depicted in handwriting when there is a pointy t-bar (horizontal line) towards the right of the t-stem.

Here is how it looks:

son today is runnin but often mistaken !

THE REASON:

Sarcasm is like a verbal dagger which is defending the ego. So if a person has been feeling insecure or inferior and do not want to face it anymore or wants to fight against it, he may use sarcasm to defend his ego. While doing so they may also hurt other's feelings. After all, they have a sharp tongue, right?

HOW TO HANDLE A SARCASTIC:

Well, if they are emotionally expressive, then you will have a hard time to handle them. As already said, sarcasm is basically used as a defense mechanism to ward off any attack to the ego. So it is best to avoid that. It is best to avoid hurting the person's ego. If you keep on mocking the person, it is evident that he would also continue to be sarcastic, targeting and taunting you.

9. THE SUICIDER

No jokes here: the suicider is a serious and most concerning issue nowadays. If someone is a suicider or self-punisher he needs you now more than ever. A suicider, as the name suggests, or a self-punisher, who punishes himself in physical or emotional forms, is apt to do that for a specific reason. You may think that he has gone crazy and requires medical attention (which of course, I would encourage!) but you can give him a first aid.

THE TRAIT:

In handwriting analysis, signs of suicide can be predicted from the leftward pointing t-bar. T-bar is the horizontal line that cuts the t-stem, the vertical line. Here is a sample of self-punishing personality:

what about

THE REASON:

The very basic reason of why a person may commit suicide is a problem, which he feels is unsolvable. If it is solvable, then the risk and stress of doing that is too much. "It is better to end the life" he thinks. Apart from the suicide, there are personalities that like to punish themselves. They do so because they have a death wish directed at self. In simpler words, an extreme form of murderous rage turned inwards. Irrespective of whether the writer is just beginning to think about self-destruction as a possible solution to his problems, or has already begun to plan it, this is always a dangerous state to be in. This feeling of self-destruction may arise from emotional pain, prolonged depression, low self-esteem, confused thinking and fear.

The self-punisher is an individual who blames himself and hates himself and is unable to cope with the circumstances which are not reasonably within his control.

HOW TO HANDLE A SUICIDER:

According to the book Men are from Mars, Women are from Venus, in order to release tension of a problem, women's behaviour is to speak it out. They would repeatedly speak the same problem to multiple people or to the same person until they feel better. They are not doing so to find a solution to the problem, but just want to speak it out and want an ear that listens.

Men, on the other hand, are quite different. Whenever some problem arises, they go into the solution-finding mode; and they do so by preferring some time alone. If they aren't able to figure it out, they would seek advice of some wise person. But beware: men do not like getting advices until asked.

To handle a female self-destroyer it is best to make her speak her heart out as much as she likes. It's best to be a good listener to do that. If you are not good at it, don't do it – you'll worsen the situation!

To handle a self-punisher, it is best not to let them be alone but give them time to contemplate, don't pressurise him to speak; that would add to the stress levels. Be with him, but do not advice until asked. Give him hope and wait for a professional help to arrive.

Last but not least, if you are bad at people skills, it's alright – accept it and be with the person, don't try to solve it – it may prove fatal! Seek professional help ASAP.

10. THE LAST MOMENT QUITTER

Have you met a person who has all the talent, all the resources to finish a project or get successful, yet when the time comes and he is about to cross the finish line – he QUITS! Strange, isn't it? But yes they do exist. A student may have studied thoroughly and might even know the answers to all the questions, yet he would make sure that he doesn't give his best. Why do they behave like this? Let's take a closer look at their personality.

THE TRAIT:

In handwriting analysis, this kind of behavior is referred to as having fear of success (no typo, yes it is "success"). These people have fear of succeeding. I know you might be wondering "Who in the hell doesn't like success? Who can possible fear from it?" Before I answer this question and explain why such fear exists in the first place, let me tell you that this trait is connected to the down-tuned y-loop that never reaches the baseline. Here is the example:

THE REASON:

You might be wondering "How can such fear exist?" Let's take a look: when such personalities are going to reach success, usually a feeling of dejection elevates, thus they get very close to success and then fail. It is evident that this trait is hard to comprehend if you yourself don't have it. In a nutshell, it can be explained that success brings changes. Generally, there is a reward for a positive result and vice versa. But people with this trait have associated failing with a positive emotion and succeeding with a negative one. When they get a promotion, they do not feel worthy of it. They turn away at the last minute and run towards a disaster. They consistently look for ways to not finish the projects.

HOW TO HANDLE A LAST-MINUTE QUITTER:

There is nothing direct that you can do to help the last minute quitter. Since they are insecure of the change, that the change which success begets can be bad, you can only help them get rid of that idea. You can make them realize that success is not associated with punishment and can reap great rewards for both him and his family.

11. THE DUMBO

Many people are tagged with the word "dumbo" now days. Let me assure you, whenever someone calls you that, be proud of it because you are going to find out some of the qualities that you possess. Basically, dumbo or dumb is a slang used for a person who is very slow at understanding concepts, ideas and situations. They understand after some time. There are various other tags that they get like "tube light" "snail" etc.

THE TRAIT:

In handwriting analysis, such personality trait is referred as slow learner – they are slow at learning, understanding and comprehending but they are good at remembering things. In handwriting, slow thinker is pertained to round "m" and "n" as shown below:

is, pretty cold
pping soon. my
n a few minute:

THE REASON:

They are slow at comprehending because these people need all the facts and figures before making a decision. They are methodical and procedural. They are so procedural that they have to read the book from start in order to understand it. If they open a book from any random page they won't be able to understand anything. Same goes with the movies – they have to watch them from the beginning to understand.

HOW TO HANDLE A SLOW THINKER:

You don't need to – just give them the time they need to comprehend. Usually, in a class they are the students who need some time or sometimes even repetition of concept to understand it completely. But on the positive side, once they have learnt or understood something they don't easily forget it.

12. THE MANIPULATOR

To be honest, when I started to research for this book, I asked a few people what is it they would like to know about what makes people do it. Majority of them said "why do people lie?" Well, your question is being answered here. In Are You Dating a Liar? There are 12 handwriting strokes depicted that can help you find if a person is a liar or not. In this book we will only be talking about one of them.

As you know, a manipulator or a liar is the one that lies and manipulates the situation. We all have been liars once in a while and also been on the victim side.

THE TRAIT:

In graphology, the manipulator trait is depicted by having two loops in the letter "o". Now, there are specific reasons and explanations of loops but we will not be covering that in this book. Whenever you see two loops in an "o", you are undoubtedly talking to a manipulator. It should be considered though, that when the frequency of such loops is low, then they may just be apt to tell white lies that do not harm anyone or may be a prankster. But otherwise, that person is a liar.

Here is how the double looped "o" looks like:

THE REASON:

Since we all have lied one or the other time, I want you to think why we would have lied that time? Of course, we lied to avoid punishment or pain. The double loops indicate that the person has a fear of telling the truth, probably because it may hurt him or someone he loves. This dishonesty may either be defensive or anti-social. If there is insecurity or sensitivity, then the writer is lying to protect himself, because he believes that other will not like him if they "really know him." On the other hand, the writer may see lying or cheating as a means of achieving some goal.

HOW TO DEAL WITH A MANIPULATOR:

Always cross-check what he says. It would not be a wise decision to trust them blindly. Bluntly saying or pressurizing them to confess won't get you anywhere.

13. THE IMMOVABLE

There are personalities that are obstinate and stubborn. You probably might have one in your family. Any names? These are the personalities that are stubborn and do not listen to anyone once they have made up their mind. They may be dominating and usually would not be open to other's opinions once they have decided. It seems like they are the decision-maker of the family.

On a negative side, these personality types may not listen to others but on the positive side, they have great determination and are immovable in that way as well. They are immune to brainwashing and manipulation from external sources once they have finalized their decision.

THE TRAIT:

This personality trait is known as being stubborn. In handwriting analysis, stubbornness is shown by an inverted-v type letter "t". It is just like taking a shape of person who is standing with his legs wide open depicting that he is immune to force and is immovable in nature.

Here is how it looks:

THE REASON:

Just like every other insecurity, a stubborn personality type also struggles to be in equilibrium. In his case, he defends his ideas. He has fear of being wrong, and don't want to be confused with the facts after he has made up his mind. Since he has taken the decision, if someone gives opinion, he doesn't listen to it because otherwise it would mean that his idea or decision was wrong, which will ultimately lead to disequilibrium.

HOW TO HANDLE AN IMMOVABLE:

As their insecurity is that they don't want to feel that their ideas were wrong, it is best not to suggest an idea at the first point. If you have to inset a point, it is best to give an impression that it was his idea rather than yours.

14. THE PRETENTIOUS

We all have probably met with this personality trait. The pretentious person is the one who pretends to be a different type of person than he really is. Only the close friends will know what he is like. So if a stranger is pretentious, you are in for trap, but not always! Pretentious people may be very nice in front of you but may backbite about you in front of mutual friends. They may be very sweet on the face, but behind your back they might be conspiring against you.

This personality trait brings a story to my mind. Once a man came to an office and asked the receptionist that he has come to meet the owner. The receptionist takes the man to the owner. When they enter the owner's office, the owner is seen talking on the phone, boasting about the deals he is finalizing in millions and billions. After keeping the man waiting for about some time he finally hangs up the phone. He asks "Yes?" and the man replies, "I have come to repair your telephone." The owner literally drowned in embarrassment. He might wanted to impress the person but at the cost of his image, and he definitely lost it by being a pretentious.

THE TRAIT:

In handwriting analysis, it is said that there can be a big difference in how a person writes normally and how he signs his name. According to this science, the normal text depicts what he is like in his personal life while the signature highlights the image he wants to project in the public. You see, it's a game of private vs public personality. It would be very common to see a drastic difference in the handwritings of public speakers, politicians and other personalities who have to deal with public, because they have to put on a mask before they appear in front of the people. They are not wrong; it is the demand of their profession.

Let's take an example: we have learnt in the chapter "THE COLD FAÇADE" that the leftward slant depicts that a person is emotionally withdrawn and would not express feelings very easily. If a person writes normal text with a leftward slant but while signing he uses a rightward slant, it is a clear indication that he has to fake his people-oriented, outgoing personality to meet with the demands of his work. He has to hide his introversion or the lack of trust in expressing feelings in front of others.

Not only this, even decorative, beautifully-crafted handwriting also reveals a person who likes to pretend and be someone else.

Here is a sample of a decorative handwriting:

Find Ring
Set Date January?
Clothing - Wedding Dress
Colors
Who will marry us?
Honeymoon.

THE REASON:

This over-large, over-flourished handwriting is also a sign of pretentious or egotism, which is another subdivision of insecurity. It clearly states that the writer needs to put on extra-bold front in order to cope up with the lack of real confidence and low self-esteem. The writer may also need attention, and doesn't feel that being himself is going to get it for him, so he opts for being pretentious instead.

Just think about it, when we decide about the sign, we always think about which sign would look the most impressive, that itself is being pretentious consciously.

In the most common front, claiming to be or presenting yourself as something other than what you are is the way to either attract admiring notice or to conceal some truth about yourself, usually a form of insecurity.

HOW TO DEAL WITH PRETENTIOUS:

Don't just get sold off! Don't get impressed with the fake front of the pretentious.

15. THE VARIETY LOVER

Have you been with someone, who may give you a lot of attention at the start but after a few months he is just not much interested in talking to you? Well, we all have met such person. They are the variety lover who gets bored very easily. They are the personalities who dislike monotony and routine work. For them, variety is the essence of life. They need change in life – place, work, people etc. Usually, you will find that they would have many friends and are very good at making friends wherever they go. On the downside, they may trust people too much and that is the reason why they get disappointed very easily.

THE TRAIT:

The personality trait of preferring variety is shown by a bulky lower-zone loop – a loop that is very wide. The loops are very long and big in the letter y, g, z. It depicts that they want variety in their activities to satisfy their insatiable physical desires. Sexually, they can be very demanding, adventurous, and often creative.

35

Here is how it looks:

to live up to my expectations of myself.
to be true to my needs while sticking

THE REASON:

This is the personality trait for which the physical gratification is the prime goal of life. Because of the same reason they are most of the times physically restless and are ready to explore new relations and experiences. This writer has excessive energy and needs more and bigger vessels to store the excessive emotion being harboured. Feelings get bottled up, because there isn't enough outlet for them; this is the reason why most of them remain physically frustrated. I usually recommend them to join some gym or exercise daily to release that excessive energy.

The key phrase here is excessive emotional and physical need.

HOW TO HANDLE A VARIETY LOVER:

Let them have what they want. They want variety, let them have it. If you keep them away from variety, most probably you will make them feel confined and the relationship would fall. Instead, if you give space, both will be in harmony. Explore about this personality – they can be really creative, ask about ideas and things they want to try. They can be great person to hang around with. But beware, because they are able to make friends very quickly and easily, don't get jealous!

16. THE RESERVED

Just like the cold façade personality trait, which seems to be non-expressive, the reserved is also a deemed personality trait for a person that doesn't crave for attention. They usually like calm places with very less people. Crowded places make them nervous and usually when they are at a party, they prefer to have their drink and sit in a corner and just observe. Even at home they prefer to latch their room's door and meet the family rarely. Generally, they are academically strong and have the ability to focus on something for longer periods of time.

People take them as reserved personality but you can explore a lot about them, if you get to talk to them and are able to make them comfortable.

THE TRAIT:

As already said, they are not actually reserved; they just prefer to stay away from crowd. In handwriting analysis, such personalities are depicted by having very small handwriting. It requires intense focus to write something small. Therefore, such writers possess the ability to focus on a single task, eliminating all the distractions.

Here is the sample:

THE REASON:

The small script is a scientist's script. It is so because many of the world's most inventive discoveries have been made by people of small script. The sample given above is that of Albert Einstein. But there is a negative side of the coin as well. This writer may also be using his work or hobby as an excuse to escape reality. It would not be wrong to say that the writer might have found something to substitute for human interaction. He runs the risk of becoming totally isolated from the rest of the world, which would ultimately mean a risk of becoming narrow-minded, incapable of growth or change.

The small writer is something of an isolationist who tends to focus all his attention and all his efforts on his own enthusiasm and to close off all the distractions – which world translates as the activities, interests, and social life of other people. He has little or no concern for the larger picture. The work which he is doing is all that matters.

It is undoubtedly great to have the ability to focus on something for long period of time but on the extreme side, it can also be a way of hiding your head in the sand, or maybe even crawling in a hole and pulling it in after you with the perception "if you can't see me, I am not there."

HOW TO DEAL WITH THE RESERVED:

Since this personality trait can have both positive as well as negative consequences, it is best to first find out what the writer is up to. Barging in or spying in is not an option, that would only make him more conscious. Trying to talk, or approaching someone without whom he may be comfortable to talk to might work. If he is working on projects – book, invention, painting etc, then it is still a healthy sign, because his energies are not going in the wrong direction. If he is not creating something with his abilities, then definitely there is a need to help him get rid of his insecurity.

Such personalities are writer of great independence who can shut out ego needs and concentrate for long hours alone. These writers are geniuses, provided their energies are channelized properly.

17. THE UNPREDICTABLE

The unpredictable personality trait is the trait in which you can't judge or be confident how the person may react to a situation. You are always in a doubt and at times hesitant as to whether to approach him or not. The unpredictable writer remains confused most the times; he has trouble making decisions because his head and the heart are always in conflict. Usually, when this writer feels insecure he withdraws into an introverted personality.

The unpredictable writers are moody in nature and can be upbeat at one moment and can feel blue the very next second.

THE TRAIT:

In handwriting analysis, the unpredictable personality trait is depicted by an inconsistent slant. It means that some his handwriting will be slanting towards the left while some of it would lean towards the right. This inconsistency in the slant shows someone who can't make up his mind about what kind of person he should be, how he should feel about others, or how he should react.

Generally, such writers want to like and trust others, but are not certain if they are liked in return, and therefore are also uncertain about how to respond to others.

Here is how an inconsistent slant looks like:

> appear to your guest like your calm and collected by having your service area set

THE REASON:

It is important to understand that this writer finds it very difficult to know how to do or how to behave with others. In a sense, he has his signals crossed: he can't grasp what other people are all about, and therefore doesn't know how to react to them, or even how to feel about them.

This unpredictability or difference in behaviour of this writer is result of what psychology calls an "approach-avoidance" conflict. In this, the writer is not able to make up his mind whether to be outgoing or reserved. It is just like a situation which has both positive and negative consequences. Because of the negative consequences, it isn't that appealing.

Another reason why unpredictability occurs in the personality is that the person might have experienced trauma in his childhood. Because of this traumatic experience they keep bouncing back to emotionally withdrawn state and hence become unpredictable.

HOW TO HANDLE THE UNPREDICTABLE:

It is hard to handle an unpredictable because you can't really say how the writer may react to the situation. He can respond in a positive way or can react in a negative way.

Whatever the situation is, try maintaining your composure. Not only this, since they are struggling with how they should perceive a situation, it is best to help them understand how they should feel.

18. THE ENDURER

Just like the cold façade or the reserved personality traits, this one too is deemed to be someone who doesn't have a heart but in actuality the opposite is true. This personality trait has the ability to face the toughest and the most tragic situation and yet they are able to come back to the normal state quite quickly. They can be rightly compared to a rubber band which can be stretched under pressure but once the pressure goes away they come back to their normal position.

To be exact, they are the polar opposite of the super-sensitive personality trait.

THE TRAIT:

In handwriting, the personality trait of a person who doesn't get affected easily by situations is depicted by a very light gentle pressure on the page. If you feel the back of the page they have written on, you would hardly feel anything. They apply very light pressure to write.

The degree of this pressure can be connected to the

involvement of the writer. So, the lighter the pressure the more uninvolved and self-effacing the writer is and usually the more personally non-ambitious as well.

Here is an example of an endurer:

THE REASON:

The reason why nothing affects them is because whoever writes this way is not likely to put a great deal of energy into anything either because he doesn't care enough, because he's ill, or because he's afraid of failure, of imposing on people, of being considered pushy.

HOW TO DEAL WITH THE ENDURER:

If you feel like this writer needs to put in extra pressure on the accelerator, start by helping him get rid of that fear of failure or the fear of being considered pushy. Assure him that this is the way it has to be. He has to direct the people if he has to get people to work with him.

19. THE NON-PRACTICAL DREAMER

The non-practical dreamer is a writer who has very high dreams, so high that he loses the touch with the reality. He lives in his own imaginative world where everything is perfect and runs according to him. But in reality it is not so. Even if you do something right at every stage, still you are bound to face some temporary obstacles.

This is a writer whom his friends consider as just the talker and not the doer, which is to an extent, true as well.

THE TRAIT:

In handwriting analysis, this personality trait is known as the visionary. No doubt they can see things not everyone can see. They have the long-sightedness. But just like hypermetropia (far-sightedness), they are able to see things in the future distinctively but forget to tune their daily activity. Somewhere they remain just a wishful dreamer.

In handwriting, the trait of non-practical dreamer is

shown by a t-bar that is above the t-stem and doesn't touch it.

Here is an example:

THE REASON:

It is true that they often just talk about what they are going to do instead of doing it. So the main reason behind this trait is that they are so engrossed with the perfect future that they tend to take the present lightly or fall victim of poor planning because of the same.

HOW TO DEAL WITH A NON-PRACTICAL DREAMER:

If you or anyone you know is a non-practical dreamer, please let them read this chapter. It is great to be a visionary, but it is equally important to take care of the daily routine so as to achieve that vision which you see in the future. As the popular saying goes, "People don't plan to fail, but they fail to plan." Try not being victim of that.

20. THE SELF-DECEITER

One of the lying strokes depicted in the book ARE YOU DATING A LIAR? is self-deceit. Self-deceiter is the person who deceits or lies to himself. When I first heard this term my reaction was "How can someone lie to himself? On top of that, why would he lie to himself?" I hope you too have the same questions in your mind.

Yes, this is the personality trait that lies to himself and doesn't want to face the reality.

Once I saw my friend's boyfriend with another girl, so I called her up and informed her. To escape from the reality, she told me that she is actually with him and I might have been mistaken. After hanging up the call, I went up to them and met the guy. It was him and I got my hands-on experience with a self-deceit writer.

THE TRAIT:

In graphology, the trait of self-deceit is depicted from the lower letter "o". When there is a single loop on the left side of the letter "o", it means that he lies to himself. If

47

this loop is rare then the trait is not so prominent but if it is frequent then definitely he frequently tries to lie to himself to escape reality.

Here is how this trait looks:

THE REASON:

As already said, the self-deceit writer is actually trying to escape the reality so he lies to himself. It means there is definitely something which he doesn't want to face. If he faces that situation or reality then he would be hurt. So the next best option is to just close the eyes and pretend nothing happened – hence, the lying.

HOW CAN YOU HANDLE A SELF-DECEITER:

Since they are struggling with facing the reality, you can help them face it. Be a support to them. Check their handwriting, a rare left loop in the letter "o" is acceptable but if the frequency is high, it is time to help him face the situation he might think would hurt him.

21. THE ANTI-SOCIAL

The anti-social is a personality trait where the person doesn't trust anyone, because of which he doesn't like to make friends. On the face, he might be friendly but deep down he may not trust them at all. He is the one who has no close friends with whom he discloses his secrets.

THE TRAIT:

In handwriting, trust is shown by the lower loops. As in the case of variety lover who has large bulky lower loops showing that they can easily trust; anti-social are just the opposite, they have a retracted lower loop such as of letters "y, z, g". This is how it looks like:

THE REASON:

Handwriting analysis is all about cause and effect relationship. A person has a retraced lower loop because he has trust issues. The anti-social writer doesn't trust people. There is lack of trust because of the fear of getting hurt. In the past, he might have being close with someone who broke his trust and left him hurt, which led to the development of fear of intimacy in him. As a result of this fear, he doesn't want to let people enter his heart.

Usually, this is someone who is just out of a bad relationship, and he is recoiling because he got hurt.

HOW CAN YOU DEAL WITH AN ANTI-SOCIAL:

Don't be pushy. The more you try to go close, the more suspicious he will get and keep you at bay. Give him his space and time. As time heals everything, he will also let you come closer to his heart. Let him take his time, and eventually he will build trust in you. Stay with him in his highs and lows to win his trust. Most importantly, never break his trust; you will make his condition worse.

22. THE DOMINANT

Have you been with a person who was just craving for control? All he wanted was to dominate – to get things done the way he wants. Either it was his way or no way. Well, that is a dominant personality trait. There is difference between being a stubborn and dominant. The stubborn is a hard nut to crack; his mind or decision can't be altered once he has made his decision. Dominant, on the other hand, wants just his ways. He should get what he wants, plain and simple.

THE TRAIT:

In handwriting analysis, the dominant trait is depicted by a downward slanted t-bar. It becomes even more cruel when the downward t-bar is pointed towards the right because then the person will make use of aggression and harsh words to take control.

Here is an example:

THE REASON:

The dominant person likes to be in control of the situation. Having the desire or need to be in charge of or to run things is what drives him. If he doesn't get that then an urge or craving of control drives the mind. This thought of losing the control of the situation is what triggers the dominant trait and makes him to tighten grip on situations and bother people.

HOW TO HANDLE A DOMINANT:

Give what a dominant wants – control. Let him control the situation, but keep driving the wheel indirectly. It is like rally racing. He wants to drive the car; this is what a dominant person wants. You can be in the co-pilot seat with map in your hand guiding him about the road ahead.

A word of caution: a dominant may not like to get instructions so you have to come clean in order to hold that co-pilot seat.

23. THE POSSESSIVE

"Why haven't you reached here yet?", "Why are you late from work?", "Why was your phone busy?", "Why were you online at 1:00 AM in the morning?" these are the questions a possessive may ask. I bet we all have been there and experienced it. This trait is what is known as being possessiveness. It is the need to "own" that other, often expressed as suspicion or mistrust of that other's faithfulness, truthfulness, or motives.

To say in a gist, when jealousy and insecurity takes over love, then emerges possessiveness. It is normal to be little jealous, little insecure and little possessive, but in an extreme form you will feel no less than being held in a prison cell.

THE TRAIT:

In handwriting, the trait of possessiveness is shown by having tight beginning loops in most of the capitals. They are so tight as if ready to hold your limbs and neck with them – a sign to beware of. Here is how these loops look:

THE REASON:

This is undoubtedly an undesirable trait to have. This trait involves an unreasonable desire to have or retain ownership of some person or object. This attitude is combined form of materialism and greed when it refers to objects and jealousy and greed in reference to other people.

This trait is triggered with jealousy and jealousy is not love, nor is based on it, it is a reactive form of insecurity.

Invariably, the writer fears the loss of someone's love. In order to keep that love with him he can be very possessive and competitive.

HOW TO DEAL WITH A POSSESSIVE:

Well, don't date one. If you have to, then don't make him insecure. Don't make him feel jealous. Make him feel special. Do not let the negative insecure thoughts come in his mind. Trust me, once insecurity takes over his mind he will never be able to see you without that insecurity.

24. THE PERFECTIONIST

There is personality trait in which the person puts in extra efforts and time to make sure that everything is in the right place at the right time. The downside of this is that they put in too much of time into this that they become inefficient. Another negative implication of this personality trait is that you are too much organized that there are no rooms for surprises. In such a scenario, if a surprise appears, say your schoolmate just bumped into you, instead of being happy you will be distressed, because instead of enjoying the moment you are worrying about the schedule and the disorganization your day will have because of this meeting/situation.

As the perfectionist bogs down to unnecessary details so they never get the job finished.

THE TRAIT:

In handwriting analysis, a perfectionist is depicted by having a very straight and rigid baseline. Even if there is a blank unruled page, they will still write in a perfect straight line. It is so even that you can literally draw a straight line underneath the text.

The person spends time and energy in putting everything in its place and reviews work trying to make it precise. In short, this person aims for perfection.

Here is how it looks:

THE REASON:

The perfectionist is the person whose baseline is too straight that it constitutes an extreme. The writer is someone who needs to believe that his guidelines are the only right answer. He never allows himself to doubt, never questions his own motives, never hesitates in making a decision. It must be nice to always be so sure of yourself! But what do you do if you are suddenly confronted by a situation in which your rules don't work? That is when they break down.

You can compare this writer with the person who is walking on a tight rope. He can't afford a single misstep, because he can't permit himself to be wrong. And as they are putting so much stress to be on line, they have a fear of losing control. When they do lose control, they panic and distress.

WHAT MAKES PEOPLE DO THINGS THEY SHOULDN'T DO

HOW TO HANDLE A PERFECTIONIST:

You can't, because they are the one who don't want to lose control. The best you can do is let them have control and don't make them feel that they are wrong because they have both the fear of losing control and fear of being wrong.

25. THE SELECTIVE LISTENER

Most of the times, I have seen relationships suffer because of this personality trait. It is fairly common to see in individuals. The trait is of being a selective listener. It means that even if you will try to explain a situation, the writer would listen and mould it in a way that he wants to listen. In short, it won't even matter if you explain something because ultimately he will only hear what he wants to hear.

It is said that relationships break because of either miscommunication or no communication. This trait is a reason for miscommunication.

THE TRAIT:

In handwriting analysis, the trait of selective listener is shown by a retraced letter "e". Here is the example:

retraced i and o

THE REASON:

The basic reason why selective listener will do this is because he has his own ideas and will only agree with you if you agree with him. So, if you do not agree with him, he can literally tune you out. In other words, this person can be close-minded.

This trait usually occurs because of too much of clutter of information or too much of command given that eventually they start ignoring it. If you come to India, you will notice that here honking is too frequent that after a week you will get accustomed to it and you won't even consciously take note of the honking. It is the same with this writer – he receives the information but never comprehends it.

HOW TO DEAL WITH A SELECTIVE LISTENER:

Since one of their needs is that they will agree with you only if you will agree, so the first and foremost step can be to agree with him or else just stop trying. In a relationship, it could be really hard to explain things to this writer.

26. THE INDIVIDUALISTIC

It is a fact that the need of attention is probably the most common trait in human nature. The need or drive to be noticed and admired for what you are or what you have accomplished. But there are people who crave for it. They need it so badly that not having this attention at some point makes them uneasy.

THE TRAIT:

When the writer feels that his own resources are inadequate (usually because he is not getting as much attention as he needs, or is getting the wrong kind), he will usually resort to some pretence to attract notice or admiration. This reaction is indicated in script by the use of some unusual and often unoriginal formation, the most common is the circled i-dot.

Here is how it looks:

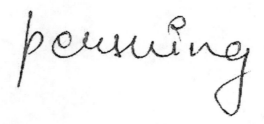

THE REASON:

This writer has invariably developed a need to be different from the crowd. I still remember when I used to have this handwriting stroke in my handwriting during my schooling. I was very careful not to be part of the audience. The same need elevates when someone is trying to stand out from the crowd. The writer has a fear of being ordinary and must call attention to him by being different in one way or the other.

HOW TO HANDLE AN INDIVIDUALISTIC:

Give them the attention they seek, otherwise they will keep tantruming for it. Understand that they need attention and if you keep them from taking it, they will feel that inequilibrium and develop anxiety and need to get that attention.

IN A NUTSHELL

TRAIT NAME – Reason behind the behavior – handwriting stroke:

• THE LOW SPIRITED – Fear of failure – Low t-bar

• THE SUPER SENSITIVE – Puts heart in everything – Heavy pressure writing

• THE IMPULSIVE – Fear of being left alone – Hard rightward slant

• THE COLD FAÇADE – Fear of expressing themselves – Hard leftward slant

• THE PRESENT LIVER – Need for approval of authority – Same height of both tall letters (t,d,l) and small letters (a,c,e)

• THE HARSH WORDER – Defending insecure ego – Pointy t-bar towards right

• THE SUICIDER – An unsolvable problem – Pointy t-bar towards left

• THE LAST MOMENT QUITTER – Fear of success –

Down-turned y-loop

• THE DUMBO – Needs all facts and figures – Round "m" and "n"

• THE MANIPULATOR – Fear of telling the truth – Double looped "o"

• THE IMMOVABLE – Fear of being wrong – Inverted "v" shaped t

• THE PRETENTIOUS – Conceal an insecurity or attract admiring notice – Overflourished handwriting

• THE VARIETY LOVER – Excessive emotional and physical need – Bulky lower loops of "y,g,z"

• THE RESERVED – An alternative for human interaction – Small handwriting

• THE UNPREDICTABLE – Heart and head in conflict – Inconsistent slant

• THE ENDURER – Fear of being pushy – Very light pressure

• THE NONPRACTICAL DREAMER – Lives in imaginative world – t-bar above t-stem

• THE SELF-DECEITER – Fear of facing the situation – Loop on the left side of letter "o"

• THE ANTI-SOCIAL – Fear of intimacy – Retracted y-loop

• THE DOMINANT – Need to be incharge – Downward slanting t-bar

• THE POSSESSIVE – Fear of loss of someone's love – Tight loops in the beginning of capitals

• THE PERFECTIONIST – Fear of losing control – Rigid straight baseline

• THE SELECTIVE LISTENER – Too much clutter of information – Retracted "e"

• THE INDIVIDUALISTIC – Fear of being ordinary – Circled i-dot

CONCLUSION

There are times when we wonder why did someone did something or behaved in a particular way. This book was my attempt to bring you one step closer to the answer. There are times or behaviors which are not described in this book but the concept of seeing the situation from the other person's perspective will help in finding the reason behind the move. After all, what we need the answer of is: what makes people do things they shouldn't do?

ABOUT THE AUTHOR

Manhardeep Singh started his journey of writing books when he was in his 11th grade. His first book *The Guideline of Life* touched so many hearts that he took the mission to change lives with his writings.

Apart from being an author, Manhardeep is a motivational speaker and handwriting analyst.

He can be contacted at **authormanhardeep@gmail.com**

NEED A KEYNOTE SPEAKER OR A WORKSHOP LEADER?

I am available to conduct keynotes, workshops and training sessions on motivation, confidence building, dream building, mastering luck and various other topics. Check out my website www. manhardeep.com to contact

LOOKING FOR HANDWRITING ANALYSIS?

You can get yours or someone else's handwriting professionally analyzed by me. All you need is the handwriting sample. Just go to my website www.manhardeep.com and follow the instructions.

Made in the USA
Middletown, DE
17 July 2025